hR.C

Troubled Treasures: World Heritage Sites

GREAT WALL OF CHINA

Cynthia Kennedy Henzel

ABDO Publishing Company

visit us at
www.abdopublishing.com

Published by ABDO Publishing Company, 8000 West 78th Street, Edina, Minnesota 55439.
Copyright © 2011 by Abdo Consulting Group, Inc. International copyrights reserved in all
countries. No part of this book may be reproduced in any form without written permission from the
publisher. The Checkerboard Library™ is a trademark and logo of ABDO Publishing Company.

Printed in the United States of America, North Mankato, Minnesota.
102010
012011

 PRINTED ON RECYCLED PAPER

Cover Photo: Getty Images
Interior Photos: Alamy pp. 5, 21; AP Images pp. 1, 12, 17, 29;
 Bruce Dale / National Geographic Stock p. 19; Corbis pp. 15, 23; iStockphoto pp. 4, 9, 10;
 Peter Arnold pp. 18, 25; Photolibrary p. 27

Series Coordinator: BreAnn Rumsch
Editors: Megan M. Gunderson, BreAnn Rumsch
Art Direction & Cover Design: Neil Klinepier

Library of Congress Cataloging-in-Publication Data

Henzel, Cynthia Kennedy, 1954-
  Great Wall of China / Cynthia Kennedy Henzel.
    p. cm. -- (Troubled treasures--World Heritage sites)
  Includes index.
  ISBN 978-1-61613-565-2
  1. Great Wall of China (China)--Juvenile literature. I. Title.
  DS793.G67H46 2011
  951--dc22
                          2010021309

CONTENTS

A Chinese handscroll tells a story on a long piece of silk or paper. It is rolled on two sticks. Readers unroll the scroll from one stick and roll it onto the other. Section by section, the scroll reveals part of the story.

Like a giant handscroll, the Great Wall winds across northern China. Altogether, the wall is more than 4,000 miles (6,400 km) long. So, you cannot see the whole story at once.

The Great Wall begins in the east at the Yellow Sea. It travels near China's capital, Beijing. It continues snaking west through numerous **provinces**. Along the wall stand numerous strongholds, or passes. The first pass is Shanhaiguan in the east. The last pass is Jiayuguan in the west.

More to Explore
Shanhaiguan means "First Pass Under Heaven."
Jiayuguan means "Last Pass Under Heaven."

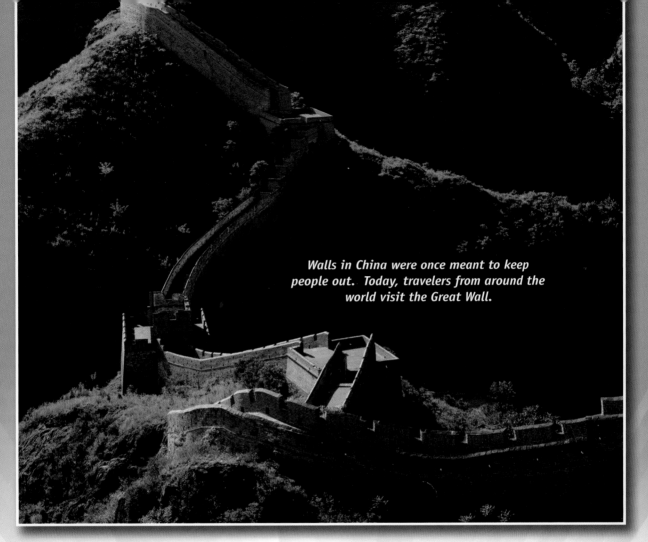

Walls in China were once meant to keep people out. Today, travelers from around the world visit the Great Wall.

The wall climbs over mountains and stretches across **grasslands** and deserts. Each section tells of the people who built the wall. Together, the sections reveal part of China's history. To make sure this story isn't forgotten, **UNESCO** officials named the Great Wall a World Heritage site.

WALLS OF WAR

Building walls is an ancient tradition in China. The Chinese built walls for the same reasons we fence our yards. Walls kept some people out and other people in. They also marked the boundaries between land belonging to different people.

Thousands of years ago, China was not a single country. The land was divided into many small kingdoms, or states. Each state wanted to protect its land from the other states. So, they built walls along their borders.

The state of Chu was located in central China. Around 615 BC, a Chu prince named Huiwang built the oldest-known wall. This state wall is known as the Square Wall.

Over time, powerful states conquered weaker states. By 475 BC, only about seven major states remained. For several hundred years, these states fought many fierce battles. This time is called the warring states period. Finally in 221 BC, the state of Qin conquered the remaining states.

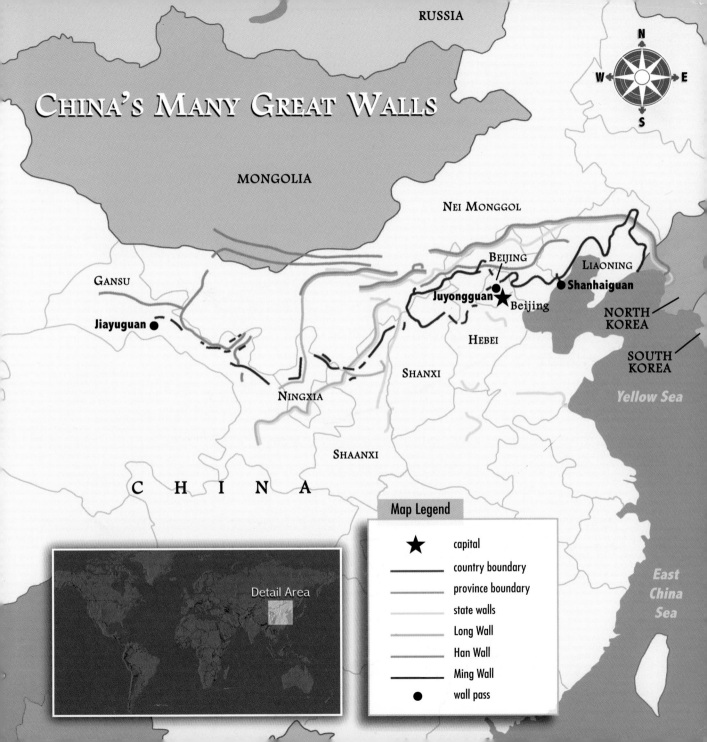

CHINA'S MANY GREAT WALLS

RUSSIA

MONGOLIA

NEI MONGGOL

GANSU

BEIJING

LIAONING

Jiayuguan ●

Juyongguan ★ Beijing

● Shanhaiguan

NORTH KOREA

HEBEI

SOUTH KOREA

SHANXI

NINGXIA

Yellow Sea

SHAANXI

C H I N A

East China Sea

Detail Area

Map Legend

★   capital

——   country boundary

——   province boundary

——   state walls

——   Long Wall

——   Han Wall

——   Ming Wall

●   wall pass

DEFENDING A DYNASTY

The Qin king proclaimed himself Qin Shihuangdi, the first emperor of China. For the first time, China was ruled by one government. It was called the Qin **dynasty**.

The emperor made many changes to unite his country. He commanded all Chinese to use the same language, calendar, and money system. He also tore down many old state walls.

During this time, nomadic people called the Xiongnu lived in the north. The Xiongnu did not farm or build cities. Instead, they moved from place to place. They hunted and raised sheep and cattle. The Xiongnu were also great warriors and horsemen. They often invaded China.

Shihuangdi needed to protect his country from these attacks. He also wanted to keep the nomads away from the settled Chinese. So, he ordered General Meng Tian to build a new wall. It became known as the Long Wall.

During Shihuangdi's rule, some workers created a clay army to guard the emperor's tomb. This vast tomb became a UNESCO World Heritage site in 1987.

Stages of China's Great Wall

The Great Wall of China is not simply one wall. It was built and rebuilt over thousands of years. Today, this work is commonly divided into four main stages. To keep them straight, the walls from each stage are known by different names.

WHAT WALL?	WHEN?	WHO BUILT IT?
State walls	615–221 BC	State leaders
Long Wall	221–207 BC	Leaders of the Qin dynasty
Han Wall	206 BC–AD 220	Leaders of the Han dynasty
Ming Wall	1368–1644	Leaders of the Ming dynasty

The Great Wall's watchtowers eventually totaled 25,000. These varied in size. Most towers sheltered at least 50 men. The largest held up to 10,000 men!

General Meng began the Long Wall by building watchtowers. Most were 40 square feet (12 sq m) at the bottom and 40 feet (12 m) high. The towers were often made of mud bricks.

Workers made these bricks by mixing water with dirt. They packed the mixture into wooden molds to dry in the sun.

General Meng built thousands of watchtowers. They were often placed two bow-shot lengths apart. This way, archers in the towers could hit anyone crossing the space between them.

Next, walls were built to connect the towers. First, workers built two narrow walls many feet apart. Between these, workers added local materials to create one thick wall.

In the **plains**, workers started with wooden outer walls. They poured about four inches (10 cm) of soil and pebbles between the walls. This layer of earth was pounded down, or tamped. Then, workers laid down twigs and reeds. They repeated these steps many times. Layer by layer, the wall slowly rose.

Desert walls were often built the same way. In some places, workers used adobe bricks to build the outer walls. Then, they filled the spaces between with dirt.

In the mountains, workers probably built the outer walls with rock. Gravel, earth, or clay filled the spaces between. Finally, this may have been covered with stone bricks.

More to Explore
China's Great Wall is sometimes called the sleeping dragon. In Chinese culture, the dragon is a symbol of power and luck.

Chinese workers have restored many sections of the Great Wall. They use methods ancient builders used, such as carrying bricks by hand.

North of the wall, General Meng built 15,000 outposts. These were like watchtowers, but they were not connected to the wall. The outposts protected important passes, valleys, and hilltops. They housed many soldiers and supplies in case of Xiongnu attacks.

To warn each other of coming attacks, soldiers used special signals. Black smoke during the day and fire at night meant danger. This system worked like a game of telephone. Signals quickly passed from one tower to the next.

Workers continued extending the wall for about ten years. Eventually, the Long Wall stretched about 3,100 miles (5,000 km). It was a great achievement. Yet, it was costly.

Hundreds of thousands of people were forced to work on the wall. This included convicts, farmers, and soldiers. The work was difficult, and the workers were treated cruelly. They endured cold, heat, and hunger. Countless workers died.

The Long Wall was like a great handscroll stretching across northern China. Sadly, it told a story of cruelty and suffering. After Shihuangdi died in 210 BC, the Qin empire began to crumble. So did the Long Wall.

The next part of the wall's story was written during the Han **dynasty**. This empire was founded by Emperor Gaozu in 206 BC. He lowered taxes and made peace with the Xiongnu. But, the peace did not last.

In 141 BC, Emperor Wudi came to power. Under his rule, China began to expand its borders. This led to more attacks by the Xiongnu. Yet, it also led to more trade.

An important route called the Silk Road developed between China and Europe. Trade along the Silk Road brought new riches to China.

Emperor Wudi wanted to protect his country. But now, he also wanted to protect the Silk Road. So, Wudi launched many attacks against the Xiongnu. Around 120 BC, he finally defeated them and pushed them out of China.

Meanwhile, repairs had begun on parts of the old Long Wall in 121 BC. New sections of wall were also built in the west. In total, Han leaders restored and built more than 6,200 miles (10,000 km) of wall. This construction became known as the Han Wall.

In the west, desert winds have eroded much of the wall. Crumbling towers are often all that remain.

In AD 25, Emperor Guangwudi came to power. He ruled until the year 57. Improvements continued on the Han Wall during this time. In 38, Guangwudi ordered repairs to four sections of the wall. This maintained China's defense against invaders. It also helped protect trade along the Silk Road.

Yet, constructing the wall and defending China cost Han rulers much money. They helped fund these efforts through taxes and forced labor. Citizens grew unhappy with these hardships. Eventually, the government grew weak. Finally in 220, the Han **dynasty** ended.

For the next 1,000 years, numerous short-lived dynasties ruled China. Some rulers added to the wall. But others neglected it. All the while, threats from northern peoples continued.

China could not defend itself forever. In 1211, Mongolian warrior Genghis Khan invaded. The Mongols ruled China for many years.

Numerous sections of the Great Wall are badly in need of repair. These sections are known as the wild wall. They are not open to tourists.

At Shanhaiguan Pass, the Great Wall extends 66 feet (20 m) into the Yellow Sea.

In 1368, Chinese peasants rose up to defeat the Mongols. One peasant became Emperor Hongwu and started the Ming **dynasty**. Again, China began to prosper.

China's third Ming emperor expanded trade. Emperor Yongle sent Admiral Zheng He on his first naval expedition in 1405. Zheng He's ship brought back riches from Southeast Asia and eastern Africa.

Around that same time, Yongle ordered that Beijing become China's capital city. This was much farther north than the old capital. But, China had become a rich and powerful country. Yongle was not afraid of invasions.

Later Ming emperors did not feel as secure. So, they closed China to outsiders. They ordered foreigners to leave. And, they stopped trading with other countries.

Still, northern peoples threatened China. From 1368 to 1644, Ming emperors defended China's northern border against invasions. To do this, they built the Ming Wall. It grew to more than 4,300 miles (7,000 km). Today, we know it as the Great Wall.

In the dry deserts of western China, Jiayuguan Pass has been restored.

CITY OF STONE

The Ming Wall extended over mountain ridges and along winding rivers. It was more than just a defensive barrier. The wall was a long, thin city.

Much of the wall was built with stone and brick. Along the top ran special walls with crenellations. These were gaps for soldiers to watch or shoot through. New drains built into the wall prevented water damage. A wide brick road also ran along the top of the wall.

Inside the wall, stairs led up to the road. There, raised platforms stood out from the sides of the wall. From these, soldiers could easily attack wall climbers during battle.

Once again, soldiers used fire and smoke signals to communicate. Beacon towers were often built close enough for soldiers to see or hear one another. The lower levels contained stables, storage areas, and rooms for soldiers.

Passes along the wall were like forts. A pass was accessed through a large gate. Above each gate stood a watchtower. It served as a command post.

Soldiers sent smoke signals from towers built on hilltops.

WALL OF RUIN

In 1644, a northern group called the Manchus seized Beijing from the Ming rulers. They established the Qing **dynasty** and ruled China for more than 250 years. The Manchus had no use for the Great Wall. So, it became neglected.

The Chinese overthrew the Manchus in 1911. Soon, the Republic of China was founded. By the 1920s, two political groups were fighting for power in China. They were the Nationalist Party and the Communist Party.

In 1949, Communist leader Mao Zedong established the People's Republic of China. Mao was not interested in preserving the Great Wall. It reminded him of poor peasants and wealthy emperors.

While Mao ruled China, the Great Wall became threatened. People removed bricks and stone to build houses. They destroyed some sections to build roads. Other areas were flooded when dams were built. Pollution wore down parts of the wall. In the west, huge drifts of sand covered parts of it. And, wind and rain caused erosion.

More to Explore
The Great Wall cannot be seen from space with the naked eye. However, radar can detect it.

During Mao Zedong's rule, many dams were built. These dams created lakes that sometimes submerged sections of the Great Wall.

TOURISM TROUBLE

The Great Wall's fate changed after Mao's death in 1976. Deng Xiaoping became China's new leader. Unlike Mao, he believed the Great Wall was a symbol of China's rich **culture**. In 1984, Deng said, "Love China, restore the Great Wall."

Soon, this work began. The Great Wall Restoration Committee raised funds to repair the wall. Most of the work took place near Beijing. There, the wall became a popular place to visit.

China even reopened its doors to the world. Today, millions of tourists visit the Great Wall each year. Money from tourism helps pay for **conservation** programs. Yet, careless visitors cause great harm to the wall. They steal rocks or leave behind garbage. Some people even write or draw on the wall.

In 2003, the International Friendship Forest opened near the Badaling section of the wall. The park works to balance tourism with conservation. It helps tourists understand the story of the Great Wall.

More to Explore
Popular sections of the wall near Beijing include Badaling, Simatai, and Juyongguan.

Hopefully, learning the wall's history will urge visitors to help preserve it. This includes taking nothing from the wall but pictures!

PROTECTING THE WALL

Like Deng, several organizations have recognized the value of the Great Wall. It is the largest military structure ever built. It is also a symbol of an ancient **culture**.

In 1987, the Great Wall became a **UNESCO** World Heritage site. Then in 1993, the US-China **Environmental** Fund was founded. This organization helps China protect its environment and culture. That includes the Great Wall.

Even with these efforts, the wall remains threatened. Less than 30 percent of the wall is in good condition. Pollution continues to cause erosion. And, people are still taking materials to build other structures. Sometimes, people even dig holes in the wall to make animal pens.

Yet, China is writing a new chapter in the story of the Great Wall. Between 2003 and 2007, much money was spent to restore and protect the wall.

Beijing has also passed laws to protect the Great Wall near the city. Laws passed in 2006 protect the entire wall from **vandalism**. Anyone caught damaging the wall now faces fines.

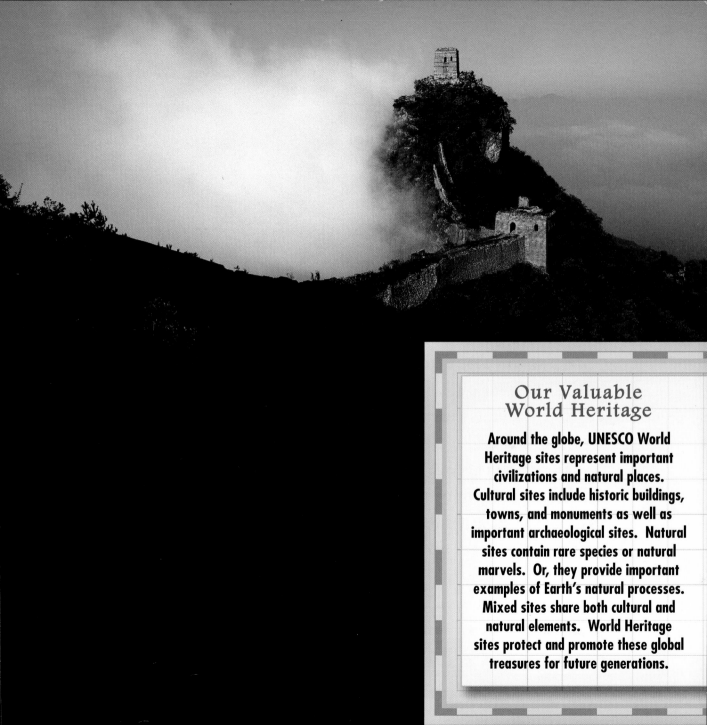

Our Valuable World Heritage

Around the globe, UNESCO World Heritage sites represent important civilizations and natural places. Cultural sites include historic buildings, towns, and monuments as well as important archaeological sites. Natural sites contain rare species or natural marvels. Or, they provide important examples of Earth's natural processes. Mixed sites share both cultural and natural elements. World Heritage sites protect and promote these global treasures for future generations.

One of the most dangerous threats to the Great Wall is the desert. While the wall was being built, much forest and **grassland** was cleared away. This provided new land to farm. It also prevented enemies from sneaking up on the wall.

But, the trees had helped keep the desert in its place. Today, about 1 million acres (404,700 ha) of China's grassland turn to desert each year. Strong desert winds erode the wall, and sands bury it. Floodwaters wash away the wall's base, making it collapse.

China aims to prevent further erosion with an ecological project. Millions of trees have been planted across the land. The area is known as the Great Green Wall. Many years ago, the Chinese hoped their wall would keep its enemies out. Today, the Great Green Wall defends against a different kind of enemy.

More to Explore

In 2007, China began a special project to map the Great Wall. Scientists discovered additional sections of the wall, making it even longer than previously thought.

No other structure represents a country's history like the Great Wall of China. Though it is threatened, this **cultural** symbol has lasted for thousands of years. China is currently writing a new chapter on the handscroll of the Great Wall. This nation wants the story of its ancient treasure to endure for years to come.

Today, many Chinese take pride in the Great Wall. It proved a fitting backdrop for many 2008 Summer Olympics celebrations.

conservation - the planned management of rivers, forests, and other natural resources in order to protect and preserve them. Conservation can also protect man-made resources, such as historic or cultural structures.

culture - the customs, arts, and tools of a nation or a people at a certain time.

dynasty - a series of rulers who belong to the same family.

environment - all the surroundings that affect the growth and well-being of a living thing.

grassland - land on which the main plants are grasses.

plain - a flat or rolling stretch of land without trees.

province - a political division of a country.

UNESCO - United Nations Educational, Scientific, and Cultural Organization. A special office created by the United Nations in 1945. It aims to promote international cooperation in education, science, and culture.

vandalism - intentional damage done to public or private property.

SAYING IT

Beijing - BAY-JIHNG
Chu - CHOO-OO
Deng Xiaoping - DUHNG SHEE-OW-PIHNG
Gaozu - GOWD-ZOO
Genghis Khan - GEHNG-guh-SKAHN
Guangwudi - GWAHNG-WOO-DEE
Hongwu - HUNG-WOO
Huiwang - HWAY-WAWNG
Jiayuguan - JYAH-OO-GWUHN

Mao Zedong - MOWD-ZUH-DUNG
Meng Tian - MUHNG-tee-UHN
Qin - CHIHN
Qing - CHEE-UHNG
Shanhaiguan - SHANG-HEYE-GWUHN
Shihuangdi - SHEE-hwahng-dee
Xiongnu - SHUNG-NOO
Yongle - YUNG-LOH
Zheng He - JUHNG-HOH

WEB SITES

To learn more about the Great Wall of China, visit
ABDO Publishing Company online. Web sites about the Great Wall of China
are featured on our Book Links page. These links are routinely monitored
and updated to provide the most current information available.
www.abdopublishing.com

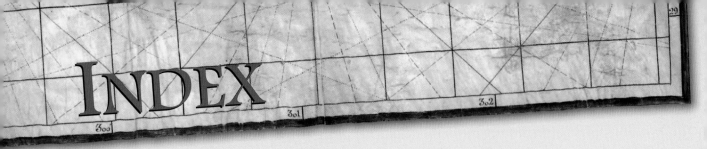

INDEX